Editorial and project management by
Shaila Shah, BAAF
Designed by Andrew Haig & Associates
Illustrations by Sarah Rawlings
Printed by The Lavenham Press, Suffolk

All rights reserved. Except as permitted under the Copyright, Designs and Patents Act 1988, this publication may not be reproduced, stored in a retrieval system, or transmitted in any form or by any means, without the prior written permission of the publishers.

Nadia and Rashid's
STORY

Children and families come in all shapes and sizes! Let's hear about some of them. When you read Nadia and Rashid's story, can you see if you can find them in the playground?

Introduction

When children are separated from their family of origin part of their very self is in jeopardy. No matter what their age or circumstances, that interruption of familiar and uniquely personal kinship ties can lead to potentially lifelong wounds. Adoption and fostering is not only about joining and welcoming, but also about grieving and losing as well as struggling and working together. Family life is never easy and new or reconstituted families have additional pressures and demands.

One of these is to help children to make sense of their often fragmented and confused experience. Their past is a crucial part of who they are and one of the key tasks for carers is to help children to integrate their past and their present. They are then able to move towards a future that builds on reality including the joys and sorrows which characterise all our stories. This task is not easy. So often the implicit message to permanent carers is to treat the child as if he or she were their own – and indeed that is necessary in order to build the quality of relationships that all parents hope for. Yet they are also asked never to forget that children are not their own – that they come from a different family with a different history.

Why this workbook?

The importance of helping children to make sense of their story is widely accepted. Each of us has a basic right to know who we are and where we come from. Children who cannot understand why they are separated will almost always take on the guilt and responsibility themselves. It is therefore vital that they are helped to make sense of their individual history. Life story books are valuable tools in this respect, but care needs to be taken that they are not reduced to little more than photograph albums. Children want to know not only what, but why, and information needs to be accurate, truthful, respectful and age/development appropriate.

This workbook is one amongst a collection relating to a number of children who are not living with their birth families. The stories each have a different scenario and it is hoped that they may act as useful triggers in a variety of settings. Experience shows that the reality of getting down to discussing and explaining is far from easy. Birth families, foster carers, adopters and social workers all struggle with the language and feelings involved. For birth families the pain and loss that is inherent in relinquishment can be overwhelming. Permanent carers can be fearful and avoidant of genuinely confronting a history which is not part of their shared experience. Social workers may be over-protective regarding difficult information and often feel lacking in communication skills. Therefore it is imperative that in order to use this workbook most effectively the reader is adequately prepared for the task.

Preparation

It is important to recognise that exploring painful and traumatic events with children evokes for each of us our own experience of loss or suffering. Learning to live with these events may be a lifelong task but we need at least to be on the journey before we can help a child to risk setting out. If there are areas of our life that remain too difficult to face we may need more time before embarking on working with children. Our fear, hesitancy or reluctance to face pain may well communicate itself to the child who will sense that difficult issues are best left unspoken and kept inside.

Some children may be overwhelmed by their experience, struggling with guilt, anger, sadness, responsibility, divided loyalties, and unsure of their capacity to survive emotionally. A sensitive, caring adult can acknowledge these feelings with the child,

Introduction

accepting but not minimising their confusion and hurt. Demonstrating a strength and resilience in the face of pain allows the child slowly to develop a sense of hope and conviction that all will be well. The stories in this series are about facts, but also about feelings, for the two cannot be separated. Adults need to be honest about their own emotions before they are able to help children with theirs.

In order to share a child's history it is essential to have as much accurate information as possible about their circumstances. Different tools may help to identify gaps in knowledge that ideally need to filled before embarking on life history work. For a fuller and more detailed account see BAAF's book, *Life Story Work*.

A word of caution

Some children with particularly difficult and traumatic histories may be unable for a variety of reasons to confront their past. Care should be exercised when children appear to be well defended and highly resistant to sharing previous experience. Sometimes such children may be receiving therapeutic help to explore painful issues and this may be a long-term process. Children – and adults – maintain their defences for a purpose and they deserve a healthy respect. These stories are potential channels whereby connections may be made, feelings shared, hopes and fears discussed and attachment encouraged. They should never be used in an intrusive way that fails to respect the child's wishes and anxieties. All adults can do is to open doors; it is the child who decides whether or not to pass through.

Using the workbook

The workbooks in this series are specific and are therefore inevitably limited in their direct application. Every story line is unique and there can be few common denominators. However, the range extends across a variety of familiar scenarios and backgrounds, and while they may require adjustment given individual circumstances, it is hoped that they may also be helpful triggers. In some cases carers or professionals may be able to use them as they stand; alternatively they may prove helpful in enabling adults to rehearse a specific story line that relates to a particular child, or children can be encouraged to note the differences/similarities between their own stories and those of the children featured.

Various tools have been incorporated into the story and the work sheets at the end are further aids to helping children explore issues and feelings. Both the work sheets and story can be used flexibly and can therefore be moved around in different combinations. It will be important for adults to consider the individual needs of each child. The workbook reflects a multicultural population and many children will require additional information concerning, for example, their racial, cultural and religious heritage; preverbal children will be more able to identify with play techniques and very simple story lines; learning disabled children may make greater use of visual content than the written word. Each child will have his or her own needs and story and the workbook is meant to be used creatively and flexibly in conjunction with the many other useful tools already available.

Birth parents, carers and social workers may find the story lines helpful to use with children as part of preparation work, within family placements, or at key times such as adoption hearings or disruption. Specific (future) stories may be helpful to families preparing their own children for adoption or fostering, stepfamilies who are adopting and those who may be helping their children to understand relinquishment of a sibling. Guardians, residential workers, family centres and day nurseries may find relevant scenarios that could be useful in their work with children and young

Introduction

people and there is an educational value in raising community awareness of children's needs and the range of situations represented within adoption and fostering.

Explaining and exploring

Life is a continual story and the task of story telling is never complete. As the child grows and develops so too will his or her understanding of their situation. Histories will need to be repeated, reworked and more carefully explained as comprehension becomes more sophisticated. It is important to use developmentally appropriate language and concepts and be aware of the need to refine and adapt material according to each child's needs and abilities. It is important to listen to children – to hear what it is they want to know and to avoid the temptation to convey too much too quickly. Stories evolve, often from short conversations about people, places, times, events. Children will often not need the elaborate explanations that adults prepare. Equally, it is dangerous to wait until children ask questions before imparting information; some never will and need permission to broach such personal issues. Such permission is not only verbal, but manifests itself in so many of our unspoken attitudes and responses to the child's history.

Visual aids such as this workbook are only one small contribution to the child's ongoing task of making sense of who they are. Direct and indirect contact with the child's family members can be a major source of information and encourage a realistic and developing understanding of what has happened and why. For permanently placed children the biggest factor will be their carer's ability to embrace both them and their history, knowing that they are one and the same. Our background may be complex and painful but sharing that experience over time within an environment of safety, acceptance and affirmation is the way to healing and emotional growth.

Nadia and Rashid's STORY

Nadia and Rashid started at Greenfield School six months ago when they came to live with Ayesha and Azeez. Nadia is ten and Rashid is seven. They are in separate classes but they see each other in the playground.

Nadia makes sure that Rashid is alright. They have both had a difficult and sad time.

Nadia and Rashid's story

Nadia and Rashid's father, Salim, died five years ago. They all cried a lot. Their mum, Pat, found it very hard to look after the children without Salim. Nadia and Rashid missed him very much. He used to tell them stories about his family in Pakistan and show them pictures of the family home.

Pat was very lonely and sad. Her family lived in Wales but they did not get along. Sometimes she was so sad that she would drink a lot and she said it helped her to forget how unhappy she was. When Pat was drunk she couldn't look after Nadia and Rashid properly. Then they felt even more unhappy.

About two years ago, Pat's friend Keith came to live with them. Nadia and Rashid tried to like him… but he didn't play with them or talk to them the way their dad had done. Sometimes he would drink a lot too and then he got very angry. Nadia and Rashid were frightened and sometimes Keith would hit them and Pat.

Mary, the **social worker**, tried to help and sometimes Nadia and Rashid would stay with foster carers. **Foster carers** look after children until they can go home or move on to a new family. When Mary came to tell Nadia and Rashid that things were better, they went home again.

Nadia and Rashid's story

One very cold day in winter, Nadia and Rashid had to wait outside their house after school because their mum and Keith were not at home. The next door neighbour, Mrs Lawrence, rang the police and they called Mary, the social worker.

Mary told Nadia and Rashid that she would find them somewhere safe to live where someone would look after them.

Nadia was scared that she and Rashid might have to go to different families. She was his big sister and wanted to be with him. If she wasn't around who would help him choose his best clothes when he went for Koran reading classes?

So Nadia and Rashid went to live with Jenny who was a foster carer.

They liked Jenny but it felt strange not to be with their family. They wanted to see their mum but were worried Keith would hurt them again. Mary told them that she would have to go to a **court** and speak to a judge about what to do.

Judges are wise people who help social workers when they have difficult problems to sort out for children.

Mary told Pat and Keith that she would ask the judge if she could find a new family for Nadia and Rashid.

Nadia and Rashid's story

Pat loved Nadia and Rashid and wanted them to come home, but Keith didn't want to live with them. Mary, the social worker, talked to Pat about the children. They talked about what Nadia and Rashid needed to be happy. Pat remembered that she had been sad when she was small and she didn't want her children to be sad. She knew that when she drank she was not a good mum and that Keith had hurt them all.

Pat decided that Nadia and Rashid would be happier with new parents. Mary told her that she would always be very special to the children and that she could still see them, even when they were with a new family.

Pat made a family book for Nadia and Rashid to read when she wasn't there. She put some old photographs of all the family in it and hoped it would remind them of the good times.

14 **Nadia** *and* **Rashid's story**

Nadia and Rashid felt very mixed up. They had moved around so much. Mary, the social worker, brought a huge piece of paper and she and Jenny talked to them about how they were feeling. The children drew lots of pictures on the paper about where they had lived and who they had met. Sometimes they were sad and angry when they talked about their memories.

Mary and Jenny told them that feelings are okay and it helps to share them with people who care for you and make you feel safe. Mary explained to Nadia and Rashid why they couldn't go home again and what it might be like to live with a new family.

The day came for Nadia and Rashid to meet Ayesha and Azeez, their new family. They already knew about them as they had seen their pictures in a book Mary had shown them. Ayesha and Azeez had met Pat and Jenny so they knew all about the children. They were all nervous at first but when they went into the garden they had great laughs on the climbing frame.

Nadia and **Rashid's story**

Ayesha and Azeez explained that they hoped to **adopt** Nadia and Rashid. And then, they could all be a family together.

Over the next few weeks, Nadia and Rashid got to know Ayesha and Azeez better and spent more time with them in their new home.

They chose wallpaper and posters for their bedroom and helped Ayesha and Azeez to put them up. It was very messy but great fun!

The children showed Ayesha and Azeez the pictures they had drawn on the big piece of paper with Mary. Mary said it had been very hard for Nadia and Rashid. Ayesha and Azeez said they understood their sad and angry feelings.

They hoped that whenever Nadia and Rashid were worried or upset they would talk to them about what was making them sad.

Nadia *and* **Rashid's story**

Nadia and Rashid moved in with Ayesha and Azeez last year. They still phone Jenny, their foster carer, to let her know how they are. They also write to Pat and see her for a day during each school holiday.

Sometimes those visits are hard. Last time Pat had been drinking and they had to leave her and come home. Ayesha and Azeez knew Nadia and Rashid were upset and helped them to write to Pat.

Living in a new family is not always easy. Rashid likes to be in charge and sometimes finds it hard that the grown ups decide! Nadia thinks a lot about Pat but Ayesha and Azeez help her talk about how she feels. They say that it's better for her to talk about it than keeping it inside.

Ayesha and Azeez don't have any other children so Nadia and Rashid have made a big difference to their lives. There is so much more food to buy, and many more clothes to wash and meals to cook! They have great fun together, especially on their family days out. And they'll never forget the last Eid (an Islamic celebration) when they had the best samosas and kebabs ever!

Nadia *and* Rashid's story

Everyone has to work at being part of a family. It's about all sorts of things. Sharing and caring. Giving and taking. Loving each other. Laughing and crying. Knowing that someone is there for you. Even after a year, Ayesha, Azeez, Nadia and Rashid are only just beginning to feel like a family.

It takes time and practice to learn to live together. Nadia and Rashid hope they will be adopted by their new *ammi* (mum) and *abbu* (dad). They're also looking forward to their first trip to Pakistan – maybe they'll see their old family home. You see, they know that their first *ammi* and *abbu* will always be part of their story and their lives.

Every story has a beginning and our beginnings are precious parts of who we are.

something to remember…

Every story has a beginning and our beginnings are precious parts of who we are. Adoption remembers beginnings, even sad ones. It gives children and grown ups a chance to share their different beginnings.

special words

A **social worker** is someone who tries to help children and their families when they are unhappy; they also try to find new parents for children who need them.

A **foster carer** usually looks after children for a while until they can go home or move on to a new family.

A **court** is the place where judges work. Adoption Orders are also made in a Court.

A **judge** is a wise person who makes important decisions about where children live and whom they should live with if grown ups cannot agree.

Adoption means belonging to and growing up with a new family when children cannot live with their birth family.

Nadia *and* **Rashid's story**

Worksheet

1 Have you lived in different places and with different people? Do you know where and when? Have you got a big piece of paper like Nadia and Rashid or a book that shows your life story? What other ways do you use to remember people and places?

_____
_____
_____
_____

2 Did your social worker talk to the judge about your story? Why? What did the judge say?

_____
_____
_____
_____
_____

3 Do you have worries like Nadia? What do you worry about and what do you do with your worried feelings?

_____
_____
_____
_____
_____
_____

4 What do you or would you find hard about living with a new family? What do you or would you like best?

_____
_____
_____
_____
_____
_____
_____
_____

Nadia and Rashid's story

5 What does being part of a family mean? These are some ideas in Nadia and Rashid's story. Can you add any more?

giving and taking

caring and sharing

laughing and crying